THE BOLO BOYS

To the Beaneys
with best wishes

Mac McIntosh.

To all infantrymen,
but especially Scots Guards,
past, present and future.

THE BOLO BOYS

THE EIGHTH ARMY - BEFORE AND AFTER

Mac McIntosh

victoria press

Author's note: my grateful thanks to Charles Thomson
for his help and encouragement.

ISBN 0 907165 23 0

First published in 1989 by Victoria Press,
50 Buckland Road, Maidstone, Kent ME16 0SH.
(Tel: 0622-52656)

Distributed by Meresborough Books,
17 Station Road, Rainham, Kent ME8 7RS.
(Tel: 0634-388812)

Typeset and designed by The River Press,
Maidstone, Kent.

Printed and bound in Great Britain by
Antony Rowe Ltd, Bumper's Farm,
Chippenham SN14 6LH.

Contents

The photos, which have not previously been published, are reproduced actual size.

NOTES ON THE POEMS

The poems have been written over the last four years. The war poems draw heavily on Mac's own experiences, but details have been changed in certain instances for poetic and/or personal reasons. The author would like to make it known that he is not a bolo boy.

Nostalgia 1926 won first prize in the Maidstone Poetry Competition, 1986.

Then and Now won first prize in The Maidstone Festival Competition, 1989.

Foreword

These poems are not pretty but they are very effective. Mr McIntosh is what would now be called, in the U.S.A., a 'dirty realist'. The dirt and ugliness of urban life and war are his subject matter - from the Hull childhood to peacetime soldiering to wartime experience and then to a Prisoner of War Camp and post-war Britain. Cecil Beaton, who photographed the R.A.F. in the Desert, said that this theatre of war was clean and healthy. He meant, I suppose, that it wasn't wet and muddy like Europe. It scarcely sounds very idyllic in Mr McIntosh's description.

In spite of the roughness of the experiences that he survived, he was and is admirable in his stoical endurance. This is life, he implies, and though there may not be much to be said for it, it has its moments and it's the only one we're going to get. This straightforwardness and honesty are the qualities that make these poems so compelling.

Gavin Ewart

Subscribers

Victoria Press would like to thank the following advance subscribers to THE BOLO BOYS who have helped to make its publication possible. Subscribers have received copies of the books numbered as below and signed by the author.

Mr DC Osborn (1), Lt-Col the Lord Burnham (2), I Smith (3), Anon (4-6), John D Semmons (7), RV North (8), Mr G Whatford (9), Mrs E Goodrick (10), Anon (11), Ken Dow (12), RE Parkin (13), John Symon (14), Ian Strudwick (15), Joan D Elsom (16-18), Sue Pullen (19), Jack Wharton (20), Edward Stow (21), Walter W Wright (22), Capt JC Fleming MC (23), Kay Topliss (24), Mrs Mary Stansfield (25), Anon (26), Mrs MJ Griffiths (27-29), Raymond C Hall (30-32), Dr GS Hodge (33), Mrs J Milton (34), Mr and Mrs JM Rudd & Family (35), LE Weeks (36), Carol Ealham (37), Joe Nixon (38-40), Anon (41-42), Anon (43), PA Godden (44-46), Anon (47-48), Mrs CJ Strudwick (49), Mr JB Emery (50), Donald Andrew McIntosh (51), Jacqueline Faulkner (52), Mr Frank Harris (53-54), M Barton (55), ML Melhuish (56), Mr VS Knight (57), RC Grant (58), Mrs J Burfiend (59), SE Harrison (60), Mr LA Dalton (61), Mrs Edna Elizabeth Parkin (62-63), Sheffield City Libraries (64-72), MM Farhi (73), Margaret Mackenzie (74-76), Jay Ramsay (77), Lord Henderson of Brompton KCB (78-80), Alan Townsend (81), John Ramsay (82-83), Mrs H Hedge (84), Terry Cordrey (85), Mary Rose Rawlinson (86), The Rt Hon Viscount Whitelaw CH MC (87), Anon (88), TV Jones (89), William G Melville (90), JM Mace (91-93), James Gordon (94), Mrs Eileen M Smith (95-99), Anon (100), Anon (101), Anon (102), Anon (103), Birmingham Public Libraries (104), Anon (105), Janet Barkway - Old Two Cottage, Deal (106-108), Nancy Whybrow (109).

Several of the subscribers saw active service associated with Mac's own. Amongst them are: Lt Col the Lord Burnham (Right Flank 1st Bn Scots Guards 1944-5); RV North (wounded near Medjez El-Bab 1943 1st Bn Scots Guards); Dr GS Hodge (MO to 1st Bn in N Africa and Italy); Joe Nixon (No 1 Coy 2nd Bn Coldstream Guards, reinforced by Scots Guards Coy); Lord Henderson of Brompton KCB (2nd Lieut Scots Guards, served with Mac at Anzio); William G Melville (3rd and 2nd Bn Scots Guards 1943-47); Capt JC Fleming MC (Scots Guards till 1942); The Rt Hon Viscount Whitelaw CH MC (Scots Guards).

Introduction

Mac McIntosh has been bombed by the US Air Force, buried alive, locked for a week in a cattle truck, taken prisoner by a 60 ton tank and very nearly executed by the Nazi SS.

He was born in Hull 70 years ago, retired in 1982 as Head of West Malling CE Primary School and now lives with his wife Marion in a quiet cul-de-sac in Maidstone. In 1938 he left his job as assistant in a gents' outfitters to join the Scots Guards. By the outbreak of World War Two he was on guard duty at Buckingham Palace. After Dunkirk he found himself digging a slit trench to defend Dartford and on exercises in the Tenterden countryside.

In 1943 he was in front line fighting with the 1st Army at Medjez El-Bab in Tunisia. By the end of the year he was in the 8th Army in Southern Italy and then landed in the first wave with the 5th American Army at Anzio on January 22, 1944. Two weeks later he was captured by a German Tiger Tank which rammed into the building above him and stopped on top of the cellar in which he was sheltering.

A few days afterwards he was caught in an American bombing raid on the German rear lines and buried in an explosion. He was pulled out unhurt, apart from heavy bruising. Following internment in North Italy there was a five-day journey to POW camp Stalag IVb in Germany in a crammed cattle truck in mid-winter. Rations consisted of a small loaf, a tin of meat and a bottle of water (supplemented by melted frost from the steel walls of the truck); sanitation was an overflowing barrel. He remains characteristically phlegmatic about the experience: "people were quite cheerful, surprisingly enough. It was slightly better than being in the front line. . . At least no one was shooting at you."

He was subsequently detailed as an orderly to nearby Heilag IVb ZW, the "show camp" which facilitated repatriation of severely wounded allied prisoners. This enabled him to smuggle home a letter attached to the stump of the amputated leg of an agreeable RAF pilot. An illicit radio followed the advance of the Russian army, until one morning it was apparent that the entire unit of camp guards had done a moonlit flit. The allied prisoners were industriously engaged in helping themselves to a supply depot in the adjoining village when they were suddenly surrounded by a passing patrol of heavily-armed SS soldiers, who took a less favourable view of the situation.

"We thought we were a goner. The SS were a trigger-happy lot. . . They escorted us back to the POW cages. They made the population take down white flags and said everybody had to fight to the last man." Heilag IVb ZW was liberated on April 24, 1945 by a Russian officer on a pony and a section of troops riding women's bicycles.

Charles Thomson

Reprinted from Kent Life

THE TIMES HEADLINES, NOVEMBER 1918

In the month when I was born
Valenciennes fell to the Canadians.
The Germans lost thousands
in its defence.

The Kaiser abdicated;
the Imperial and the Prussian thrones
were gone forever.
The First Great War was ending:
an artillery duel
where the infantry died
on uncut wire
and horses and men sank
in the all-engulfing mud
that was for ever Flanders.

Did poppies bloom
on that eleventh day?
Were the beats of millions
of aching hearts
heard in the silence
of that first eleventh hour
just for two minutes?

We who are old no longer care;
for those days are now
distant folk memories.
In the month of my birth
there were no potatoes for Londoners
and beer cost sixpence a pint.
David Lloyd George declaimed
and another George retained his stature
as the House of Windsor.

Only 140,000 were unemployed.
Total war meant total work.
Maybe peace would bring
a land fit for heroes.
Survivors of the holocaust
swelled the unemployment queues,
and within a year were allowed to sell
matches in the streets
and beg or sing for food.

NOSTALGIA 1926

Was it only yesterday
I held my Grandma's hand
as the full-tide lapped and slapped
against the seaweed-bearded piles
supporting the ferry pier?
And watched
as grunting deep sea trawlers
raced for the nearest berth
in St. Andrew's dock,
where fisher wives with wicked sharpened knives
sliced cod and halibut and hake
and husbands' throats, to hear them talk;
retaliated with fluent Anglo-Saxon words
at the whistling home-bound crews.

High-sided Baltic timber boats,
pit-prop-loaded to funnel height,
thump-thumped their ponderous way
to vast unloading quays.
A Holland boat discharged
twin, coal-black, matching mares
for funeral hearses;
and boxed tomatoes, cucumbers, lettuces and eggs.

In 'hoss wash',
down from where I watched,
gentle, giant Clydesdales stood patiently
and snorted with delight
at being scrubbed.

A string of lighters floundered by,
close-cutting corners,
swinging with the tide
and swilling oily waves
against the sculling coggie-boat
pushed hard against the run
by sweating bummer, late for work.

And as we slowly wandered home
across the City Square,
a melancholy, handcuffed line of men
shuffled past, to court and fines
or even jail
for rioting the previous day.
We took a clanking, swaying tram
with windows wire-netted
(the rioters had smashed the glass),
and then I fell asleep
against my Grandma's arm.

SATURDAY NIGHT OUT

White naptha lamps hissed frantically
like one-eyed cobras hypnotising prey
and chased long shadows in and out
the flapping canvas of the roadside stalls
in the fretful late November night.
These kerbside treasure troves
were magic places to my childish eyes,
counters stacked with sheer delight -
nougats, fat minty rock
and brightly coloured sherberts,
red piled apples, tangerines, banana hands
and nuts of every shape and size
were tempting to the touch.
"You keep your fingers off."
A scarf-muffled, throaty voice
gave warning of some pending doom
and hastily I hid my hands.
Tin soldiers, bright, in stolid lines
and wooden forts with cannon
that could shoot out peas,
tinselled dolls with yellow hair.
Masks of Indians, Chinamen and Ghosts
brought shivers down the spine.
Old books, old clothes. Old man and wife
with dripping noses, black-rimmed nails,
smiled toothlessly and made me quail.
The butcher's chopping block and flashing knives,
skinned rabbits and huge meatless bones
goaded me to run;
but aunty's hand held firm
and popped into my mouth
a giant everlasting ball I sucked for half the night
and mingled with chips and peas from greasy paper bag.

The ever-moving wayward restless crowd
filled all the rain-washed paving slabs
and bustled half across the road
where spluttering Fords honked cautiously.

There'll never be such nights again.
The worst that happened was trodden toes
or face pressed hard against
some fat old lady's bum.

THE TRAVELLING MAN

In the mean streets off Hessle Road
stood meaner shops
whose catalogue of goods for sale
would turn Woolies
into Harrods any day.

Old women, always tenant, never owner,
in their floral pinnies,
hair stitched tight with clawing rollers,
shoo'd the cats off stale bread rolls,
flicked mice droppings from the counter
onto bales of rabbits' straw,
and gossiped, with a nasty cough,
to penny-pinching customers.

The bell vibrated a dozen times;
fly-catchers swung like long thin lumps of Spotted Dick
and from the cavernous back
she waddled in, with stockings sagging,
slippers clacking on the unscrubbed boards.

"What you want?"

As uncompromising as any union boss.

My case clicked open.

"Not today."

"But look at this.
It's new from France.
Here have a smell."

A dewdropped nose sniffed sparingly.
"Sorl right but I can't sell that."

I showed displays
of aspirins in plastic packs,
a dark bottle with even darker stuff inside
that cured all colds

and eased the piles,
burnt off warts
and did things to underarms
that scared me stiff.
She shook her head:
"I gave a dose of that to Bert; I haven't seen him since."

Pink lint wadding, cotton wool,
celluloid patches for blackened eyes,
Dr. Whatsit's little pink pills.
She looked thoughtful and sighed,
"my Angie tried them and finished up with twins."
Corn pads.
She nodded,
"a dozen of them."
(Good Lord, I've got an order.)
Lipsticks, mascara, nail varnish.
She examined each with with sausage fingers,
wedding ring embedded in the fat.

Liquorice and cinnamon sticks,
tinctures of this and that,
gripe water, fever cures,
talc and bath salts, sherberts of every shade,
if you like them yellow, green or red
to coat your tongue.
She had a pound of each
to make a tidy profit,
screwing every ounce into
a cone of old newspaper.

I almost clicked the lock
when, leaning forward, conspiratorial,
her piggy eyes close to mine,
she whispered,
"any Frenchies?
I'll take a gross.
We sell a lot round here."

ROYAL DUTIES

Have you ever noticed the groove in the pavement
outside the railings of Buckingham Palace?
I helped to make it with my spit-and-polished boots.

I stamped from sentry box to Constitution Hill
on a two hour stint,
peering through my bearskin, ready to Present Arms
to any of the local royalty.

We'd turn out the full Guard to salute the Blues and Royals
as they trotted past to Horse Guards Parade.

It was August, just before war broke out.
It was sweaty hot.
The scarlet tunic fitted like a glove and the rifle,
heavy as lead, clung to my shoulder.

Salutes and Presents came and went to Admirals and Generals
and blokes in silk top hats,
and to an A.T.S. girl who gave me a saucy grin.

Crowds. You'd never seen so many people
and never would again
till Victory Day.

I kipped in the Palace, in the Guardroom to be exact,
but you never really slept.
Two on and four off for twenty-four hours
killed any thoughts of sleep.

On the 'twelve to two', in the early hours on the front gate,
you could expect a meat pie perhaps
from a tired, homeward-bound, ever-generous pro,
who'd stand and chat
and tell you how much she'd earned.
She sometimes had a beer, but that was chancy.
The sergeant might smell your breath.

All this no longer happens.
The posts are inside the railings
and new grooves are being worn
by other spit-and-polished army boots.

And at the end of the Guard?
God, how your feet and back ached.
But you marched with bags of swank to the shrill of pipes
back to barracks, a bath and a walking-out pass.

3.9.39.

It was just another day, another humdrum day,
and Pirbright sat in solemn Sunday ease.
Dan and I were due on guard
and brass on blancoed webbing
needed just one more rub.
The sun sat warm on both our arms
as we lent against the black old wood
of huts erected perhaps in World War One.
They smelt of age and creosote
and scrubby weeds bounced gently in the breeze
against their unprepossessing sides.
Across the range a bird shrilled out her late summer song
and Dan stared up.
"Yon's a lark," he offered and I didn't doubt his word.
Poor lark.
The whizzing buzz of countless 303's
would counterpoint her autumn tunes,
and we who sighted down the range
at targets, round and fat as any German pigs,
would aim a little off when bird fluttered into the air.
A sudden flurry woke us up.
"The news is on. Yuse lazy sods come in and hear."

A silver-padded voice crackling through our ancient speaker
told us what we knew we'd hear.
"It's war again. It's us and them again,"
the old sweat joked. He'd joined in late 'eighteen',
knew all the ropes - and how to knot them. . .
"We'll be in France by end of month, ye ken.
But watch the Frenchy gels;
they've knockers like drill pigs' backsides.
Maybe we'll all be dead by Christmas."
His weathered face broke into smiles.
"Nemind. That's what they pay us for."
A siren flung its warning cry across the blue sky
obliterating lark song and we stared
towards imagined planes.
The sun iced over, darkening all our thoughts;
then we laughed and, shrugging into webbing,
tramped off to do our first wartime guard.

3rd September 1939. This photo was taken immediately after the announcement of the declaration of war. It shows Mac (left) and friend about to do their first guard duty 'on active service'.

WAR GAMES

The umpire with his major's crown
and white armband on his sleeve
indicated his decisions.

"You are dead
and you are dead;
and you've been wounded -
bullet in your arm;
and you've been wounded -
shrapnel in your leg;
this position's overrun;
that position's destroyed."

We grinned and sat around;
for us the scheme was over.
All we had to do
was watch the others
at their play.

And one day came the real thing.
It was just as arbitrary,
but the dead were dead for ever,
the wounded screamed
and we didn't grin
when we were overrun
by Hermann Goering Grenadiers
who didn't wear white tapes.

TROOPING

Vomit
all over the Biscay-battered troopship
rivet-rattling through January gales
with two thousand of us
battened down like battery hens
in spaces for five hundred.

Vomit
on decks where squaddies
spent day and night in the scuppers
wave-washed, rain-washed, hosed down
by indifferent weather and sailors.

Vomit
in the passageways
where we slipped and cursed our way
to boat drills or anti-sub watches
and stared at our escorts
as they raced and plunged
around our sodden, sullen ship.

Vomit?
some had nothing left to vomit,
only green-biled lips and white-furred tongues.
Would they ever feel alive again?
Any battlefield was better than this hell-hole
where we neither ate nor slept, just struggled
against this rocking horse of a ship
and its fatty bacon and plum duff.

THE DAWN ATTACK

We lay behind Banana Ridge all day
watching the German spoiling attack.
They came in with Mark Four tanks;
our seventeen pounders burnt them up
and the artillery stopped the infantry.

None of us slept that night.
We shivered in our greatcoats.
About 3 a.m. I had some tea laced with rum,
I couldn't face the stew.
We cleared our guns and spat and hawked a bit.
I had a leak behind a cactus bush
and then it was time.

White tapes through the minefield
led us to the start line.
I was fifty yards behind the first wave
when a German fired high in the dark.
I crouched lower
and hoped I wouldn't stop one in the guts.

Then we were among them.
I squeezed the trigger
and felt the gun bounce in my hands
and someone screamed.
Fragments of grenades
hissed over my head.
We bombed and gunned one hole after another.
Suddenly all the noise stopped
except for "Kamerad, Kamerad",
and I saw that dawn was breaking on the hills.

I stank.
I hadn't done it since I packed in nappies.

We set off at a run
but the mortars had our range;
a burnt-out tank was handy cover
so we dived around it for shelter.
Our Intelligence Officer
lay behind a track
checking his chinographed map.

There was tremendous bang
at the front of the tank
and it ground backwards down the hill.
I screamed a warning -
too late.
As the tracks screeched over
there were bits of him sticking to it.
His head burst like a grapefruit
before he could even cry out.

We scraped off what was left
into a gas cape,
took it to the communal grave
the pioneers had dug
and dropped it in.

We took all our objectives by late afternoon.

THE TANKMAN

I'll never forget that tankman.
We had to get him through
a narrow hole in his Churchill.
Bits of flesh stuck to my hands
and he flopped onto the ground
when we finally dragged him out.

There was a smell of roasted flesh
and pieces peeled off leaving bare bones.
His uniform had burnt away.
There was no face you could recognise;
it was brittle and black like charcoal.

We wrapped him in a gas cape
and humped him to a hole
and dumped him in.
"Hard luck, mate - better you than me"
were our final words.

I scrubbed my hands in petrol
to get rid of the stench.

THE BURIAL PARTY 1943

There was a roasted tankman
and twenty of our lads to bury.

They lay there in the sweaty midday sun,
maggots screwing in their stinking flesh
and flies, droning in the burning heat,
sucked at mouths and eyes; theirs and ours.
It made you puke and think, "this might be me".

Their AB 64's, one I.D. disc, rings and watches
were collected into bags
and parcelled up for wives or parents to cry about,
unless some light-fingered bastards at H.Q.
did a bit of 'borrowing'.

We dug a hole in the sun-baked, stony earth.
It was big enough, or so the padre thought
and he ought to know.

We laid them in a neat row. As neat as you can
when arms and legs have 'gone absent'.
I jumped in to straighten one or two
or the hole would have to be made larger.
We hadn't enough blankets
so we covered some with groundsheets or gas capes
and the quartermaster wrote these off as 'lost in action'.

One poor sod had been run over by a tank
so we scooped him up in a gas cape
and dumped him with the rest;
a jellified nasty squelchy mess.

Grey faces gaped up to the sun;
'walking-out' fingers, stiff for ever now,
pointed down to scuff-toed boots,
whilst the padre droned on endlessly
and I watched an enemy spotter plane
droning, too, across the shadowless sky.

No firing party. No last post.
We filled the hole in
and the drops of blood from our blistered hands
were the only tears that were shed.

SWANSONG FOR SAMMY

We was close up to their positions, me and Sammy;
Jerry was dug in just over the brow
of this bloody great Bou.
How we got up there I never could remember,
but covering smoke and the mortars
had bombed us in to where we was.
We had crept and clawed and shot and spat
and chucked a few grenades for luck.
"By Christ it's hot," gasped Sammy,
"I could sink a pint of bitter right now.
Let's have a fag - you got a match?
And keep your bleeding head below the rocks."

We lay and sucked the smoke deep into our bellies
and 'watched our front' as careful soldiers should;
and cleared our throats of muck and sand
(we could hear the Jerries spitting too).
"They're near, "whispered Sammy, "where's the sergeant?"

"I'm over here and are you two O.K.?
We're going in with the bayonets, are you ready?"
"Bloody hell," whined Sammy, "we're knackered;
how about a Naffi wad and a cup of cha?"

"It's now," snarled the sergeant, "get ready,"
so finally we fixed our 'knitting needles'
and then we heard Jerry give a shout.
"Kamerad, hey, Kamerad," he yammered
and a white flag sprouted out of the ground.
"Surrender," muttered Sammy, "that's not like them;
I bet they're trying something on.
But what the hell, stay here, I'll have a shufti."

So up he gets and tells them Kamerads
to "get over here and bloody quick."
I watches Sammy and didn't see no German
until this ripping Schmeisser sounded off.
Sammy staggered, coughed once then sprawled out.
And the Africa Korps officer laughed,
"verfluchten Englander" or some such crap.

My rifle bounced once and I hit him
right between his cocky, sneering eyes.

THE NIGHT PATROL

This patrol had to be like a gang bang
the sergeant said. In and out fast;
it didn't matter who got hurt.
The C.O. wanted a prisoner or two
and six of us had to do the raid.

We each had a Tommy gun, grenades,
a knife and some cheesewire
(the last two for a quiet piece of work).
We set off with stockings over our boots,
blackened faces and cap comforters.

We knew where the Germans were.
We'd been there before.
There was plenty of cover in the Wadi
(just the place they'd set an ambush)
so we went through it like a dose of salts
and came up behind this outpost.

We slithered in quick and used our knives.
'Boozy' Brown tried the cheesewire
and we had to hold the Jerry down;
he died like the rest of them -
except one.
He was a bull-faced Gefreiter
who was half-inclined to take us on
till 'Chalky' jammed a Tommy gun in his guts.

We booby-trapped the dead
and hustled Bull-Face and our shadows
back to the lines.

A ninety minute job.

1943. Two photos found by Mac on the body of a German soldier
in North Africa. They show captured British soldiers under escort,
possibly in France earlier in the war.

THE BATTLEFIELD

The German attack had begun
just before dawn.
The barrel of the Bren
was much too hot to touch
so my number two pissed on it
and I filled magazines
and reset the sights,
whilst the smoke screen lazily dispersed.
There must have been twenty or more
dead and wounded Germans
who'd been caught in the cross-fire
and I gave them another burst,
just to make sure.
We'd stopped them in their tracks,
me and my number two
and a dozen or so Churchills
that littered the field,
some with their exhausts
still belching out smoke
and their six-pounders swinging to and fro
across their arc of fire.
A Besa suddenly snarled from one of them
and I watched the tracer dip to the far hill
but there was no reply.
One tank, not far behind us,
was 'brewing-up'
and the stench of roasting flesh
made me gag.
My number two turned his stomach up
all over my legs and boots
in the bottom of the slit trench.
What with that and my own sour sweat
we really stank.
The sharp crack of mortar shells
made us keep our heads well down,
with only a quick peep now and then
to make sure no crafty Germans
were trying it on.
The battle haze soon went
and we could see

what was left of 'B' company -
not much.
We lost some good lads that day
but the Germans lost a lot more.
I went over to those we had killed
just in front of our position;
they'd got too close for comfort
before we wiped them out.
I nicked a Mauser and a pair of Zeiss
as well as a couple of gold rings -
no good to any of them now
and some other fly squaddy
would only do the same.

We were relieved that night
and had a hot meal of bully
and mashed spuds and tinned peas
with rice pudding for afters.
We never even washed our hands.

R.A.P.

(Regimental Aid Post)

Bloodied shell-dressings littered the ground
and flies covered them in their thousands.

These dead and wounded were my friends;
I'd laughed and joked with them an hour ago
but now their greying faces, flecked with pain,
rebuked my movements as I tried
to bring them temporary ease
with morphine needles in their arms.
I marked the dose in yellow crayon
on sweating foreheads.
The dead? We marked their tags and emptied pockets.
In weeks to come a grieving wife or sorrowing mum
would turn these treasures in their hands;
all that was left, except memories.

The M.O. smiled his gentlest smile
to soothe the pleading fear
in dying eyes;
"you'll be alright; we'll sort you out."
We did.
We buried him with twenty more
before the day was gone.

We cringed into the ground
when the German barrage crunched close by.

"I'm blind, I'm blind"; a panicked screaming voice.
He was.

And lying close, a neuter sobbed,
whose testicles
were sliced by slithered steel.

Four small neat holes stitched across guts
slowly oozed
and confirmed another due to die.

Sucking gustfully for air
a wounded head seeped out its brains.

Bullets, 'S' mines, shells and fire
all took their toll.
Could human flesh withstand such punishment?
It had to; we moved further up
to collect the debris of another fight.

THE BOLO BOYS

Every battalion has them
but H.Q. seemed to collect most;
they were cocky and fly, real chancers,
but I envied them, 'fiddles and all'.

They were dodgy and into all rackets,
remembered King's Regs line by line;
you'd find them in all the soft numbers,
well-hidden from N.C.O.s' eyes.

They had coupons for rations and petrol,
really stung you for warrant or pass;
they always had money for boozing
and dodged all the dirty fatigues.

The military police often nicked them;
they did jankers without any moans;
the occasional stretch in the 'glasshouse'
seemed to keep them in touch with their mates.

There was one in my section called Benson.
A Churchill brewed·up just behind;
he was in like a flash when it cooled
and returned with a packful of tins.

Because all the labels were scorched off
our grub was a right hit-and-miss.
That day we scoffed peaches for breakfast,
topped up with 'bangers' and peas.

But what did it matter for all that?
The dead didn't want what he'd nicked.
To Bolo Boy Benson it was scrounging,
which is 'army' for sharing all round.

No doubt they were there at Corunna
and up on the Veldt near the Boers;
Mons and El Alamein knew them;
Falklands would have its fair share.

Bolo Boys never seek trouble;
it finds them without too much fuss.
They've always an eye for the main chance.
Ours finished with the best demob suits.

SHORT-ARM INSPECTION

Every once in a while, on a wet windy day,
the M.O. decides without further delay
to have an inspection of short-arms (not small arms) -
the difference is obvious, so let's have no qualms.
Licentious soldiers are called to parade
to make sure they are healthy: a complete charade.
The sergeant-in-waiting says, "right, drop your pants.
Let's see what you've got there." He leers as he rants.
The M.O. inspects, with obvious distaste,
a range of varieties down below waist.
"Take that man's name, sergeant (a dose of the crabs)
and that man too (God, it's covered with scabs)."

FOUR DAYS LEAVE

Between the end of one campaign
and the beginning of the next
we had four days' leave.
Jim and I borrowed a fifteen-hundredweight
and arrived at the Rest Camp,
a villa on the beach just outside Hammamet.

A 'drill-pig' was running the place;
his 'tache quivered
and his face did a split job when he saw us.
"Just the place for you two.
This is an ex-knocking shop.
There's no trade now, but I reckon
I'd make a good Madam."

"Garn. You'd overcharge and have first pick
and you'd have them all
standing to attention on the job."
His grin widened
"you two up in room three."

I flopped on the bed and stared at the ceiling
and couldn't believe my eyes.
I've seen a few dirty pictures in my time
but this lot - Christ Almighty.
It made the Kama Sutra look like Enid Blyton.
There were all fifty-seven varieties
of donkeys and supermen;
it made me jealous.

Jim grinned.
"I saw an exhibish like that in Cairo -
Aussies and matelots wanted to join in.
I finished up in 'dock' with my scalp stitched.
Look."
"Go on, you're taking the mick."
"No, honest. These Arab women know all the tricks."

I still didn't believe him
but it was hard to sleep that night.

It was the only leave I had in three years.

SEABORNE LANDING

The L.C.T. that thumped us along
from Naples to Anzio
finally sat its backside on a sandbank
half a mile from the landing zone;
a German railway gun tried to zero onto us
but we were spitting distance out of range.

The rocket ships
as well as half the British
and American navies
gave a Brock's display
and shattered most of the town.
It was empty except for women and kids,
and some poor sods from the farms.

We got moving once again
into dodging L.C.I.s
and plunged, thigh-deep, into the sea
for a one-way trip to the beach.
We moved across the sandy shore
like oil down the side of a Castrol can
and dived for the cover of a pine wood
to sit and bite our nails away
for endless griping days,

until we ran into some H.G.G.s,
a poxy, dangerous lot.
It was blood and guts for the glory boys
and a bleeding fright for the rest.

War ain't such a marvellous thing -
too many shells day and night;
and even if you manage to dodge
the bits that are flying around,
you get the shakes and wish to Christ
you were back home, safe in bed.

THE TIGER

Tiger, Tiger, hidden tight,
in the barn there on the right;
Panzerführer standing by
watching Shermans, squints an eye.

You were forged for the 'master race',
stolid monster, lacking grace.
Yet what can match your 88?
Seventeen pounders, in a fight.

And what turret and what track,
that twists and turns, both fore and back.
When your cannon starts to shoot
'goodbye Sherman'; it 'brews' the brute.

What the recoil, what the flame;
what the horror of your name.
Flat trajectory pierces steel;
burning flesh begins to peel.

When the smoke screen blows away
you are there to bar the way.
Piat missile blasts your skin;
that'll make the squaddies grin.

Tiger, Tiger burning bright
in the barn there on the right,
Panzerführer, hair alight,
screams for help; he's lost his sight.

ROLL-CALL

"Call the roll, sergeant."
"Sah."
He pulled the tatty paper from the pocket on his thigh.
"Adams. Who's seen Adams?" He was the first to die.
The bullets tore his guts to bits; he screamed, but only once,
and dropped like a bag of spuds. He was the company ponce.
"Bulford. Where is Bulford? Bulford are you there?"
"I'm over here with Stanford; he's gone and stopped a pair."
"A pair? Use your shell dressing and get that Bren down here."
Chapman's gone - and Duggan - and Edmonds wants a beer.
"Shut up, you stupid bastard, get digging and watch your
        front."
Name by name he called them: "Macallister, MacIntyre,
        Corporal Brunt,
Crookshanks, Williams ("here Sarg"). An endless nominal roll.
And when he'd finished calling they realized what a toll
had been extracted for the taking of a lousy little farm
full of stinking cow shit in a crumbling rotten barn.

Seventy men had started off between the marking tapes.
Thirty were left, excluding the dead wrapped in their gas
        capes.
The sodding rain had started and they cursed their rotten luck.
"Wish I were back in Egypt," muttered Jenkins, company cook.
"What? with poxy bints, and shite-hawks ready to tear your
        pills.
And sand and flies and Rommel's lot looking out for easy kills.
No. Good old Itie whores are much more to my style.
Next leave I'm going to Naples to make myself a pile,
flogging soap and blankets." The sobbing scream of a mortar
        shell
had them diving for cover again. Then the barrage gave
        them hell
and another ten were torn apart. Edmonds never got his beer.
And the sergeant and the officer found the end of their army
        careers
in puddles of blood.
And the nominal roll?
Did it matter any more?

REQUIEM FOR AN INFANTRYMAN

You ain't no officer material, mate,
as you take the oath and sign
your very own warrant of death.
No work, so what the hell,
the army ain't too bad
and you get fed and clothed and paid.

You square-bash, do some sentry-go;
you fire a weapons course
and learn to spit and polish.
You might make corporal one day
if you keep your nose clean.

You ain't no blue-boy
with a fancy Spitfire to clean the sky.
You ain't no bell-bottomed matelot
on a sea-sicking battleship, washing the seas.
You're just a foul-mouthed, khaki P.B.I.
with a rifle, a bayonet and a spade, mate,
for you to dig your own trench, or grave.

And up the line you sweat your fears away
listening to the shells and hearing the worms cry;
cringing against bullets and smelling the wild grass roots
and tasting the bile with that last swig of rum.

You see the dead in piles, mate,
and hear the screams of the dying;
your shoulder rocks to the recoil;
you smell roasting flesh in tanks
and go numb to the shock of bayonet against bone
and your bowels and bladder spill.

You die, fast or slow, mate,
crumpled in the stinking mud
that sucks at your boots and face
and draws you into its wet embrace.
You poor bloody infantryman.

1944, Italy. Mac shortly before being taken prisoner.

P.O.W. LIFE

Stalag IVb

Two lumps of bread,
three smallish spuds,
a mug of cabbage soup.
It livened up your buds.

Ten grammes of jam
and ten grammes of sugar
and ten grammes of margarine.
It certainly was a bugger.

These were our rations
to feed us for a day.
We managed, with a fag or two,
to keep the wolves at bay.

First we lost a pound,
then we lost a stone.
It wasn't long before
we were all skin and bone.

Food from the Red Cross.
Their parcels saved our skins,
from Canada and Argentine
in neatly labelled tins.

The high barbed fence
and inner trip wire
gave the sodding German guards
another chance to fire.

If anyone stepped
too close to the line
they didn't give a tupp'ny damn
for us British swine.

They often shot the Ruskies
just for fun
and left them hanging on the wire
stinking in the sun.

"Deutschland über alles."
You trigger-happy gang;
when the war was over
you'd be the ones to hang.

LICE

We were hungry and cold
in our stinking prison camp,
and lice arrived in their thousands,
selecting the weakest first to taste blood,
copulate and lay eggs.
We scratched and scraped, then scratched again
but lice, like lovers, stay close for warmth.
The threat of typhus made us sweat.
It took the Ruskie prisoners in their hundreds
and who were we to expect exemption?
Hot knives and lighted candles killed the lice
along the seams of shirts and pants.
We burned them by the thousand.
But every day another crowd had found us out.

From starvation, pestilence
and especially lice, Good Lord,
save all war prisoners.

CHANCER FRED

His name was Fred; a chancy bloke
who deserved an Iron Cross.
Once a week at the very least
he nipped across the wire
to satisfy a lusty Frau
and quench his own desires.

He did his stuff for himself and us;
he kept us full of grub.
Sauerkraut and pickled pork,
hard black bread and ersatz jam,
bratwurst and cheap cigars
and, once, some home-smoked ham.

He used a plank to cross the wire
to meet his randy Frau
and the posterns never fluffed his game,
until one moonless night
the stupid berk fell off his plank
and a sentry screamed out "Scheist".

He also fired a round or two
and the searchlight got switched on
but Fred was gone. He was back in bed
in his hut with the rest of us.
The Germans made a rapid count.
Feldwebels can't half cuss.

Fred's lucky star was kind to him
and no one hauled him out
to spend a hungry week or two
in the cooler. What the hell,
he was out again the following night;
with a chancer you never can tell.

51

MY HOME IN GERMANY

1945, Heilag IVb ZW, the 'show' camp for the repatriation of severely wounded allied prisoners, where Mac was a P.O.W. orderly until liberation.

LIBERATION DAY

The first Russian officer I saw
was riding a Shetland pony
with his feet
trailing on the ground,
and his men rode women's bikes.
I learned his name was Stephan.
(The patrol were Mongolians.)

I met him later at a vodka party.
He was so drunk his eyes glared redly,
but his laughter was infectious.
He was in love
with a sergeant in the Military Police.
She wore stainless steel false teeth.
Her name was Anna
and she worked as a traffice controller.

Through a Russian-speaking G.I.
they told me that for them
the war had been a bitter time,
their lands and homes destroyed
and far away.
But for us
the war was almost over.
(The same words had been used
by the German officer who captured me.)

And me?
I had spent
the last two years
in a German propaganda camp,
the outside world open to us
only through a radio
screwed to the underside of a table.
The Germans never found it
but how we sweated when
the Unterfeldwebel banged his fist on the table
to emphasize some delicate point.

We showed it to him
after liberation.
He scratched his head and laughed,
"you British".
And we felt betrayed
when he was hanged, with other guards,
deep in the woods.
Who did it and why, we never knew.

THEN AND NOW

Remember the war years?   The Battle of Britain?
The vigils on Romney on dead winter's nights?
The threatened invasion?   The barbed-wire defences
rust-spiking the beaches from Margate to Rye?
The black-out, the Dorniers, V1's and V2's?

I dug trenches in orchards and guarded old houses,
played war games in Woolwich, made mock raids on Bexley,
fired rifles at Hythe and got married in Sidcup.
Went off to the war and returned to the drabness;
the rations were meagre and Maidstone was dingy.

But, heavens, what changes the years have accomplished.
M2 and M20; TVS is now here;
we're losing the orchards; the hop fields are dying;
the gipsies are missing; East-Enders have gone;
and I haven't seen glow-worms for many a year.

From Dover to Calais there'll soon be an alley -
instead of a Garden we'll be a backyard.
Our children will 'parler' and 'sprechen' like natives.
'Colorado' and rabies will add to our fears,
with bombing and hijacks - and rail strikes as well.

Condemned by our nearness to Brie and baguettes,
part-English, part-Gallic, we'll flavour our tables
with croutons and garlic and fizzy French beer.
A county of transits and Euro-transporters
with 'Follies' in Tonbridge and 'Cancan' in Deal.

VIRGIN NUDISTS

Mummy didn't like it
but Daddy didn't mind,
when I told them Pru and I were
thumbing to a nudist camp
down in southern France.
We had only just left Benenden
(you know, where Prinnie Annie went)
and we fancied something different
from California or the Seychelles,
which is where we usually stay.

Actually it was smashing,
but I wasn't very sure
about stripping all my clothes off.
(The Headmistress wouldn't approve.)
Daddy is the only one
to see me skin to skin;
I was in the bathroom showering
when he came barging in.

Mummy had some words to say:
"darling, don't you think
it's time you turned the key there;
after all, you're getting big."
In fact I'm rather small,
but there you are - conventions.
I bet Daddy didn't mind at all.

Pru and I decided
to strip down piece by piece;
first we slipped our bras off
and warmed our boobies in the sun.
Then we dropped the bottom bit,
lay face-downwards on the sand
and wondered who would take a chance
and chat US up for once.

We had only been there moments
when I heard this sudden flop,
so I turned my head - and gasped a bit.
He was huge and old and fat
(a bit like Daddy if I remember).

Pru and I, we laughed at him:
he was a German lump of dough.
And off we dashed and joined some boys
who were playing with a ball.
(I almost said "balls"
but that would be non-Benenden.)
It really was such smashing fun.
We enjoyed ourselves a lot,
and now I know what the boys have.
They're better than fat old men.

THE INTERVIEW ROOM

I ain't done nothing wrong, Miss, 'onest.
Do you really like the colour of me 'air?
I get the dye from Baker's down the 'igh Street;
I like this green but sometimes do it pink,
especially when I've got to earn a pound or two.
Me mum? She often 'elps me put the dye on
and washes out the towels when we've done.
Me dad? 'E just sits and watches telly.
'E never says a word, 'e never does.
'E's been on the social three years now
and all 'e does is watch the racing and the snooker
and bashes mum when 'e's had a pint or two.

You what? I left school last term
and was glad to see the back of that.
Those bleeding stuck-up teachers
never learnt us nothing.
I couldn't understand a word they ever said.
Where do I work? You must be joking.
None of us will ever get a job.

Ooh yeh. The clinic fixed me up on the pill
cos me mum thought me dad fancied me,
but he could never get me on me own.
Me and me sister Mary and our Joey
all sleep in the same bed.
Joey, 'e's nine now and quite a little towrag
and knows it all and sometimes tries it on,
but we clout him and push him out,
though I reckon that won't stop him fairly soon.

Smoke? Yeh, course I do, 'ave done since I was ten.
Grass? Cor blimey, Miss, I shouldn't tell yer
but yeh, we roll 'em at the disco;
I packed up sniffing glue - it made me nose all scabby.
But Ernie, 'e's my boyfriend, 'e's on the needle
and now 'e's bleedin'-well 'ooked.
It costs a bomb, at least twenty for a shot.

The money? Well like I told yer,
I earn some, you know, just knocking
on back seats in the multi-storey.
Ernie don't give a tuppenny damn
as long as 'e can see the pusher
who flogs stuff in the shed behind our flats.

The old man? Well I didn't do it.
I 'eard 'im yelling murder in that alley
and saw some blokes. They was swearing rotten
but 'oo they were I couldn't give a toss.
'E's dead? Well e' should of coughed up shun't 'e?
Then there wun't 'ave been no aggro would there?

Me the look-out? Come on off it.
I was only standing there, just waiting for a touch,
you know, a few minutes on the backseat of a car.
What! You've picked up Ernie and 'e's coughing,
well the rotten bleeder, that's just what 'e would do.

Sign here? This is my statement!
You're holding me for further questioning!
'Ang on. I want to see a Brief.

Can you let me have another fag?
Please. . .

NORTH OF WATFORD

There are towns in the North with odd sounding names,
like Brum and the Pool, Wigan and Hull.
They're full of odd men in cloth caps and boots
who wipe noses on snot-coated sleeves.
They talk in dialects strident and coarse
that aren't fit for you southerns' ears.
They mine for the coal and smelt all the iron,
build bridges and ships, pollute air with their smoke.

They enjoy weird concoctions of food for a start,
like polonies and pikelets, black-puddings and tripe,
cow-heels, pigs trotters, sheeps brains and the like,
hot-pots and brawn, stewed rhubarb and rice.

They exercise whippets and pigeons all day
whilst they chew on their Pontefract cakes;
there's sawdust on't floor of most of t'pubs,
where best bitter is supped by the pint.
And the wives knock back bottles and bottles of stout
to keep their vast figures in trim.

Cricket's more holy in Yorkshire and Lancs
than ever it is down at Lords.
Old Trafford and Headingly, Trent Bridge as well,
are battlefields studded with scars
from bowlers like Truman and old Billy Bowes,
and seamers with plenty of swing;
while tricky slow turners with fullness of flight
send down Chinamen, googlies and ones that go straight.

Their football is tribal; it's more of a war,
especially when playing down South.
But the roar from the Cop doesn't leave any doubt
what they think of the ref and t'other team's fans.
But fiercest of all is the North's rugby league:
it's played with brute cunning and stealth.
They bash on and crash on and flay in the mud
like hippos enjoying a mid-winter bath.
And the songs in the tubs when last whistle's gone
remind them of what is to come.

So when next you get past Biggleswade North,
have a care what you eat or you say.
Use 'buggers' a lot and bags of 'by gums'
and remember that old Yorkshire lay
"that if thou wants anything done for nowt,
think on, thou must do it thisen."

WHISKY

In a state of contemplation
pour a dram of single malting,
with a partner or without one
gently sip the hours away.
Tongue the taste of malted barley,
roll the tang of peaty water,
stored in casks for years maturing.
USQUEBAUGH (colloquial Gaelic)
Water of Life or Highland Spirit,
born of moors and ancient places,
golden warmth in sourly weather,
winter's ease or nightcap pleasure,
old man's love or old maid's peace.

Scotland's cream for all and sundry
on Hogmany or Robbie's evening.
Shrill the pipes and reel the dancers,
feel the glow of sweating faces,
taste the past; tomorrow's headaches
payment for indulgent pleasures.

A POXY LOT

We was knackered, me and Shafter and Daniel;
we'd marched across half of bleedin' France
and then back again and our stomachs rumbled all the time.
I still had a bit of chicken leg in my pouch
and a crust of bread, but my leather bottle was almost empty.
I'd got the French pox from a farmer's lusty wench,
and so had Shafter and Daniel. We shared everything.

Henry fancied a Frenchie throne and we was there
to try and catch Burgundians. We'd chased the Lollards
in England and now we was chasing the Catholics
in Flanders. At least that's what our captain said.
We didn't give a toss for any of 'em. Just give us grub,
a willing lass and a warm fire
and we'd fight old Nick his very self.

We'd marched fair fifty miles and most of it
without our shoen. Barefoot we went through blind dark
        forests
and waded the open marshy lands, our bows unstrung
across our backs and thirty arrows each to aim.
No loot as yet. No clanking silver cups or jewelled caps.
No fancy lace, no capes of fur to swap for hayloft favours.

We came across the Frenchie lot; my God there were
        thousands.
Their army stretched across the plain and we had only
        hundreds.
They all had horses, damn great Flemish mares.
They waved their banners, shook their swords
and screamed their Frenchie oaths at us.
We said nothing, strung our bows and listened to our orders.
Our captain said we'd loose our shafts when they were
one full flight away. We'd do it together. We knew the drill;
we'd done it all before.

A thousand arrows left the strings and then a thousand more.
Their horses fell in hundreds kicking and screaming in the
    mud
and lords and kings in heavy armour kicked and screamed as
    well.
They was easy prey for likes of me and Shafter and old Dan.
We slit throats like gutting pigs, and looted all we could.
Gold and silver, flashy ruby rings and strings of pearls;
they was a creeping, bloody poncey lot. What a day we had
    of it.
And, when we'd done them all, me and Dan was richer by any
    measure.
Shafter had his face sliced off so we was even richer.

We'd heard our Henry yapping on about St. Crispin's Day,
but we was hungry and wanted wine and women to share our
    booty.
St. Crispin's   all a load of cod when you've smelled
the blood and fire of war and finished off the screaming
    horse and man
who hadn't long to live; and slung dead mates in shallow pits.
Our dead was only ten companies, but the French - by our
    Lady -
they'd lost a lot. We left them on that stinking field
at a place called Agincourt
for fox and crow.